BEAU PEEP BOOK 17

From The

©1996

Express Newspapers plc

Research by
Mark Burgess

Published by

Pedigree
BOOKS

Pedigree Books Limited
The Old Rectory,
Matford Lane, Exeter,
Devon EX2 4PS.

under licence from
Express Newspapers plc.

ISBN 1.874507.66.X
Printed in Italy

KU-755-428

Recommended
Price

£4.99

BP 17

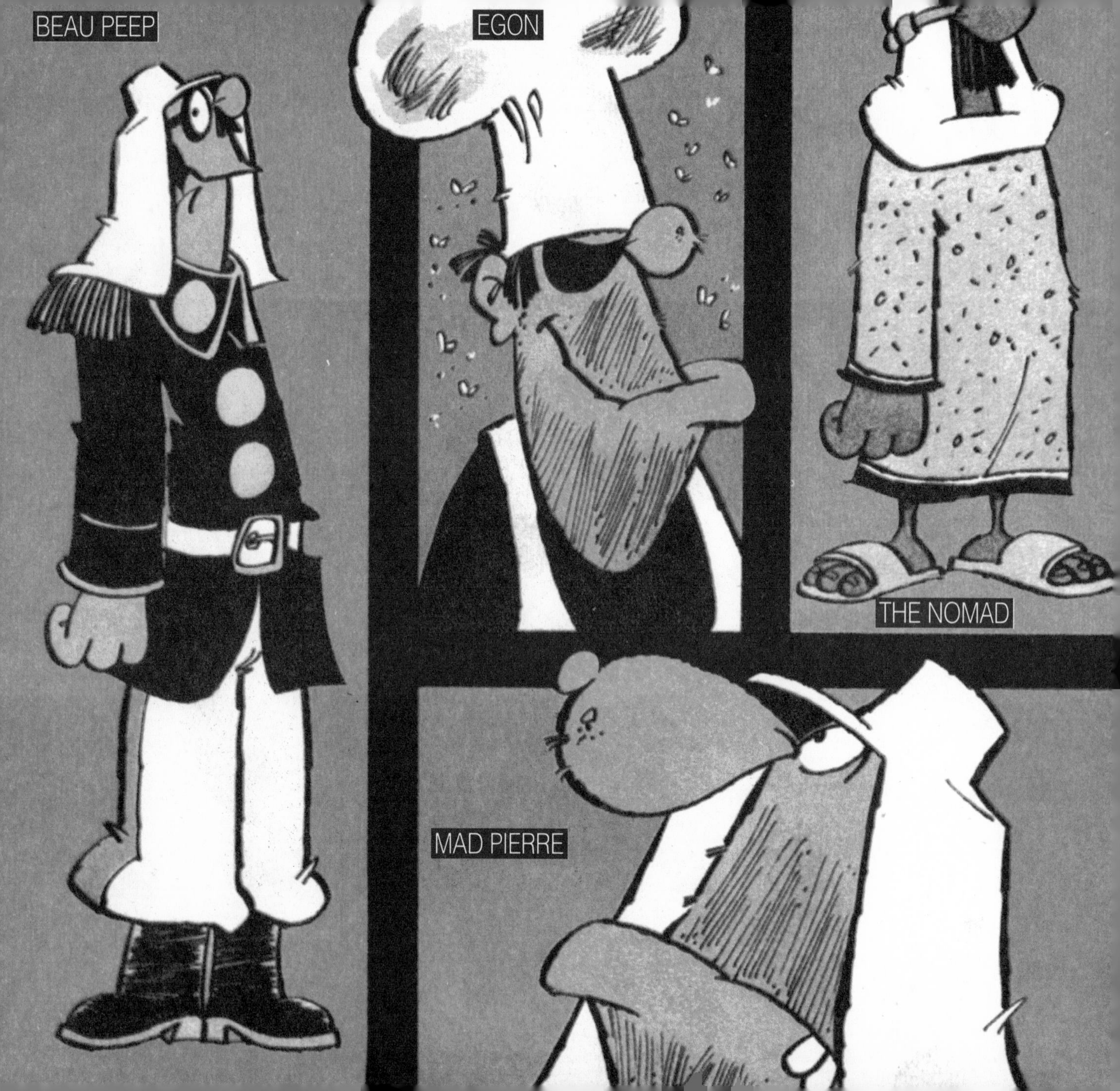
BEAU PEEP
EGON
THE NOMAD
MAD PIERRE

DENNIS

HAMISH

SERGEANT BIDET

COLONEL ESCARGOT

THE VULTURE

Roger Kettle (writer) and Andrew Christine (artist) pictured at a recent Cartoonists' Award Function, where "Beau Peep" was nominated in the "BEST COMIC STRIP ABOUT THE FOREIGN LEGION WHERE THE HERO HAS A MOUSTACHE AND GLASSES" category.

It was third.

THE ADVENTURES OF LEGIONNAIRE
BEAU PEEP
FROM THE DAILY STAR

I'M LOOKING FOR SOMETHING FOR BEAU PEEP'S CHRISTMAS...

HONEST ABDUL

4396

WELL, I'VE GOT SOCKS, HANKIES, NICE GENTS GLOVES...

HAVE YOU GOT ANY LEAD PIPING?

I'D LIKE TO BUY SOMETHING HUMOROUS FOR BEAU PEEP'S CHRISTMAS...

HONEST ABDUL

4397

...SOMETHING THAT WOULD SUIT HIM PERSONALLY.

DO YOU HAVE A JOKE BOOK FOR PEOPLE WHO CARRY FORTY POUNDS OF UNSIGHTLY FAT?

LET'S SEE...I NEED TO BUY SOME CHRISTMAS CARDS.

HONEST ABDUL

4398

I LIKE THE TASTEFUL, TRADITIONAL SORT.

GIVE ME TWO DOZEN OF "SANTA'S TOPLESS JINGLE BELLES."

I'M STILL NOT SURE WHAT TO BUY FOR BEAU PEEP'S CHRISTMAS.

HONEST ABDUL

4399

MAYBE I COULD GET HIM AN L.P.?

HAVE YOU GOT "TWENTY PARTY HITS FOR PEOPLE TOO UGLY TO GET OFF WITH ANYONE"?

WELL, I THINK THAT'S MY SHOPPING DONE.

HONEST ABDUL

4400

ALL THOSE WONDERFUL LITTLE SEASONAL TOUCHES THAT CAPTURE THE SPIRIT OF CHRISTMAS.

AND ENOUGH MISTLETOE TO SNOG THE FACE OFF AN ELEPHANT!

THANK GOODNESS YOU TOLD ME ABOUT "SAINT IDIOT DAY"!

EST ABDUL

4481

I WOULDN'T HAVE KNOWN TO BUY ALL THESE THINGS FOR MY FRIENDS.

I'D HAVE LOOKED A RIGHT IDIOT!

YOU'VE NOT BEEN SHOPPING AT HONEST ABDUL'S AGAIN!

4482

HE ALWAYS SELLS YOU EXPENSIVE RUBBISH THAT NOBODY CAN USE!

NOT THIS TIME!

I BOUGHT A SPANKING NEW TURNIP JUICE-MAKING MACHINE!

YOU TOLD ME YESTERDAY WAS "SAINT IDIOT'S DAY" AND I SHOULD BUY PRESENTS!

HONEST ABDUL

4483

I WANT MY MONEY BACK FOR ALL THIS RUBBISH YOU SOLD ME!

I CAN'T—TODAY IS "SAINT NO RETURNS DAY"!

BEING A WRITER IS SO FRUSTRATING!

THOSE STUPID PUBLISHERS DON'T RECOGNISE ORIGINAL TALENT WHEN THEY SEE IT!

HOW COULD THEY POSSIBLY REJECT MY CLASSIC "TARKA THE HEDGEHOG"?

4484

MAYBE I SHOULD WRITE A BIOGRAPHY.

PEOPLE LIKE TO READ UNUSUAL UNKNOWN FACTS ABOUT FAMOUS PEOPLE.

"William Shakespeare — Playwrite, Poet, Snooker player."

4485

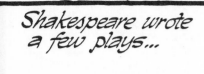
Shakespeare wrote a few plays...

...but people don't realise what a good snooker player he was.

He wrote "Romeo and Juliet pot the black."

4486

William Shakespeare was obsessed with snooker.

Playing badly would make him very depressed.

He wrote "Macbeth" after going in off the pink.

4487

IT'S EASY WRITING BIOGRAPHIES OF DEAD PEOPLE.

4488

NOBODY CAN CHECK THE FACTS TO PROVE YOU RIGHT OR WRONG!

Shakespeare had a sardine tattooed on his bottom.

"DEAR SIR, I RETURN YOUR RIDICULOUS BIOGRAPHY OF WILLIAM SHAKESPEARE."

4489

"IT IS OBVIOUS YOU HAVE NOT DONE THE SLIGHTEST BIT OF RESEARCH."

"HE DID *NOT* DISCOVER AMERICA AND HE DID *NOT* DATE ANNIE OAKLEY."

Dear President of America, I think your country would benefit from having a King...

...a noble man of bearing who would handle the position with dignity.

slip me a million buckeroonies and I'm your man.

THIS IS THE SECRET OF SUCCESS...

4508

...SPOT AN OPPORTUNITY THAT EVERYONE ELSE HAS MISSED AND EXPLOIT IT!

Dear President of America, I notice your country doesn't have a King.

I'M APPLYING FOR THE JOB OF KING OF AMERICA.

4510

I'LL HAVE TO ASSURE THEM THAT I'M CAPABLE OF PERFORMING ROYAL DUTIES.

I can wave.

Dear President of America, I would like to be King of your country...

4511

...a symbol of decency, a figure-head of benign authority...

...the owner of a "Get-into-Disneyland-free-forever" card.

WHAT'S THE CORRECT, FORMAL WAY TO ADDRESS THE AMERICAN PRESIDENT?

UM,..."MR. PRESIDENT," I THINK.

Dear ~~Boss Yank~~,

4512

I'VE BEEN WRITING TO VARIOUS WORLD LEADERS.

4513

THIS ONE'S TO THE AUSTRALIAN PRIME MINISTER.

"DEAR SIDNEY OPPRA-HAUS,"

THE DUCK-HUNTING'S A BIT SLOW AT THE MOMENT.

I KNOW! I'LL TEMPT THEM OUT WITH ONE OF MY CUNNING DECOYS!

THE THRILL OF THE HUNT!

THAT SPORTING BATTLE OF WITS BETWEEN MAN AND BEAST!

BETWEEN "MAN AND HEN" DOESN'T HAVE QUITE THE SAME RING.

YOU SEE, DUCK-HUNTING IS REGARDED AS A NOBLE SPORT.

BEING A FAST-FLYING FOWL, THE ODDS ARE SEEN AS FAIRLY EVEN.

SO, IN ANSWER TO YOUR QUESTION—YES I'M SURE SOMEBODY WOULD MIND IF YOU HAD A POP AT A CAMEL.

SERGEANTS' EXAM
HOW WOULD YOU ORDER A DISCIPLINED WITHDRAWAL?

PLEASE USE LESS THAN TEN WORDS.

"Run, Run, Run, Run, Run, Run, Run, Run, Run,"

4571

SERGEANTS' EXAM —
WHAT SIZE SHOULD A BAYONET BE?

Just big enough to put your pint on.

Hang on — I thought that said "Beer-mat."

4572

I DEMAND TO KNOW WHY YOU FAILED ME ON MY SERGEANTS' EXAM!

THERE WERE 50 QUESTIONS ON THE PAPER — YOU ONLY ANSWERED THE FIRST 12.

YOU SHOULD HAVE WOKEN ME!

4573

"*Desert love Poems.*"

A collection of romantic verse which touches the heart with a tender caress.

Also called "Snogging Sahara-style."

4580

HOW DO I GO ABOUT WRITING LOVE POEMS?

I KNOW! I'LL USE MY OWN PERSONAL EXPERIENCE!

4581

"*Desert Love Poems.*"

I love you, my darling Pamela.

Even though you look like a camel-a.

4582

Panel 1: "Desert Love Poems"

4583

Panel 2: I think of you each hour I wake, And I'm filled with a terrible ache.

Panel 3: Your name, it was Mary, You worked in a Dairy and you called me your "Little milk-sheik."

Panel 4: SNIFF! THIS IS A VERY MOVING POEM I'VE JUST WRITTEN.

4584

Panel 5: IT BEAUTIFULLY CAPTURES THAT MAGICAL MOMENT WHEN LOVERS KISS FOR THE FIRST TIME.

Panel 6: SNIFF! "MIND MY TONSILS" IS MY BEST YET!

Panel 7: DEAR SIR, THANK YOU FOR SENDING US YOUR BOOK "DESERT LOVE POEMS."

4585

Panel 8: SADLY, THERE IS VERY LITTLE DEMAND THESE DAYS FOR WELL-WRITTEN POETRY.

Panel 9: SO IMAGINE TRYING TO SHIFT THE PILE OF DUNG YOU WRITE.

COOKERY BOOKS— PAH!

RIP!

NO MORE SHALL I BE SHACKLED BY THESE CULINARY CHAINS!

I'VE ALREADY PROVED YOU CAN MAKE OXTAIL SOUP FROM ANY OLD ANIMAL'S TAIL!

EGON'S ON SOME SORT OF CULINARY CRUSADE.

HE SAYS PEOPLE SHOULD EXPERIENCE EXCITING NEW COMBINATIONS OF TASTE.

WHAT'S THIS?

DUCK-FLAVOURED SHORTBREAD!

EGON, I'M ALL FOR A BIT OF EXPERIMENTATION.

INDEED, I LIKE TO THINK OF MYSELF AS QUITE ADVENTUROUS AS FAR AS EATING GOES.

HOWEVER, I REFUSE TO EAT A BOILED EGG WITH RHUBARB SOLDIERS.

A MYSTERIOUS STRANGER APPROACHES.

HE IS TALL AND HANDSOME.

HELLO, ASTRO!

DAMN—THE VERTICAL HOLD'S ON THE BLINK AGAIN!

SLAP!

I CAN GIVE YOU A COMPLETE PALM-READING FOR £50.

ER...THAT'S A BIT ON THE EXPENSIVE SIDE.

HOW ABOUT A PALM-BROWSING FOR A FIVER?

YOU HAVE MADE YOUR SELECTION FROM "THE WARRIOR CARDS."

"ZARG THE DESTROYER" SHOWS THAT YOU ARE FEARLESS AND INVINCIBLE IN BATTLE.

HOWEVER, YOU'VE PICKED "GORDON GIRLIE-PANTS,"

PEEP IN THE DAILY STAR

BRITAIN'S BRIGHTEST NEWSPAPER

"AUTOGRAPH-HUNTING CAN BE A LUCRATIVE HOBBY."

"THE SIGNATURES OF TOP AMERICAN STARS CAN FETCH FORTUNES."

Dear Mr. Sinatra, Frankie, baby!

MON: 4658

Dear Frank Sinatra,

When I was young I learned to speak English by listening to your records.

That was even before I'd learned to tie my shoo-be-do-be-doos.

TUES: 4659

Dear Frank Sinatra,

Have you ever thought of switching to country and western music?

I only mention it because I think "Hank Sinatra" has a nice ring.

WED: 4660

Dear Frank Sinatra,

How about slipping a few Bucks "My Way"?

Get it? "My Way"! I thought you might like a chuckle as you write the cheque.

THUR: 4661

Dear Frank Sinatra, I read that your autograph is worth a lot of money.

I think this is a sign of the money-grabbing times we live in, don't you?

If you agree, please sign and return the enclosed form 37 times.

FRI. 4662

STILL NO REPLY TO MY LETTER TO FRANK SINATRA!

ME, HIS BIGGEST FAN! I'VE GOT ALL HIS RECORDS, KNOW EVERYTHING ABOUT HIM!

THAT'S THE LAST TIME I WRITE TO "OL' BLUE EARS"!

SAT: 4663

MY NEW DISGUISE HAS ARRIVED AT LAST!

MON: 4706

I'LL BE ABLE TO SNEAK UNNOTICED INTO THE FORT AND ATTACK THEM.

WHO COULD POSSIBLY SUSPECT I'M NOT A HARMLESS CHRISTMAS ROBIN?

I'LL BE IN SIGHT OF THE FORT SOON.

TUES: 4707

I HAVE TO CONVINCE THE SENTRIES THAT I'M A HARMLESS CHRISTMAS ROBIN.

I'D BETTER START BOB-BOB-BOBBIN' AROUND!

THE CUNNINGLY-DISGUISED ASSASSIN HAS ARRIVED AT THE FORT GATES.

IN THE UNLIKELY EVENT OF THE SENTRIES BEING SUSPICIOUS, I'D BETTER MAKE SOME ROBIN NOISES.

CHEEP! CHEEP! OR MAYBE CHIRRUP! CHIRRUP!

WED: 4708

YOUR LIFE-LINE IS QUITE LONG...

THUR: 4726

...YOUR INTELLIGENCE-LINE IS ABOUT AVERAGE NOW, ROLL UP YOUR SLEEVE.

BOY, THAT UGLY-LINE JUST KEEPS ON GOING!

I SEE GREAT JOY IN YOUR FUTURE...

FRI: 4727

...AND POUNDS! LOTS OF POUNDS!

A GREAT BIG WOMAN CALLED JOY IS POUNDING YOU!

NOW WE COME TO THE GOOD NEWS IN YOUR HOROSCOPE.

SAT: 4728

AT LAST! COME ON THEN — WHAT IS IT?

A PHOTO OF YOU BEING STRUCK BY LIGHTNING WILL WIN A PRIZE!

I'VE GOT GREAT HOPES FOR THIS NEW MAGAZINE I'M WORKING ON.

IT'S AIMED AT MEN WHO TAKE A SERIOUS INTEREST IN HISTORY.

PART ONE HAS A FREE BLOW-UP DOLL OF JOAN OF ARC.

THUR 4768

WHAT DO YOU THINK ABOUT MY ARTICLE ON CLEOPATRA?

WELL, I IMAGINE A COUPLE OF STATEMENTS YOU'VE MADE WOULD BE DIFFICULT TO PROVE HISTORICALLY.

LIKE HER NICKNAME BEING "CLEZZA."

FRI 4769

WELL, YOUR ARTICLE CERTAINLY PUTS A DIFFERENT SLANT ON HISTORY.

I PARTICULARLY LIKE THE BIT ABOUT CAESAR MEETING CLEOPATRA...

"...CHECK OUT MY PYRAMIDS, JOOLS BABY." SIGNED, CURVY CLEO."

SAT 4770